Katharine Short

Reflections

A BOOK FOR MUMS

A LION BOOK

Copyright © 1981 Lion Publishing

Published by
Lion Publishing
Icknield Way, Tring, Herts, England
ISBN 0 85648 340 0 (hardback)
Albatross Books
PO Box 320, Sutherland, NSW 2232, Australia
ISBN 0 86760 256 2

First edition 1981
Reprinted 1981

Photographs: Lion Publishing/David Alexander 35, 58, 63;
Jon Willcocks 10, 30, 46, 51; Jean-Luc Ray 15
Illustrations: Bridget Appleby 13; Simon Bull 45;
Margaret Chamberlain 6, 18, 25; Garet Cousins 4, 61;
Ron Fearns 43, 53; Janet Good 29, 32, 36; Jenni Lofts 38, 49

Printed in Singapore
by Tien Wah Press (Pte) Ltd.

'Here I am, with my arms full
of today's lunch and tomorrow's breakfast.
Something to make the furniture shine,
the bath sparkle, the washing whiter than white.
Something to solve all the problems of life
—except the problem of me.'

Wendy Craig as Ria,
in the BBC TV series *Butterflies*

Contents

Just food?

MY friend's four-year-old was having a party. 'What sort of cake are you making?' I enquired, knowing her skill as a cook.

'Sausages!' was the short reply.

I looked surprised.

'It's the only thing she likes,' my friend explained. 'She eats sausages, draws pictures of them, makes them in plasticine—and I bet she dreams about them too. In fact,' she observed glumly, looking at her roly-poly daughter, 'she even looks like them.'

As every housewife knows, food takes up the major part of the week's work. Shopping for it, preparing it, clearing up after it—we always seem to be eating. And for most of us, a permanent diet of sausages would be a bit repetitive.

Thank goodness some of today's men make excellent cooks, as all my sons' friends prove, with their exotic foreign foods. My neighbour's husband gives her one Christmas present every year that I envy—he does all the Christmas cooking.

But these special occasions are not the hardest part. It's

the daily, endless providing of more ordinary fare that drains the spirit and makes you feel that food can be boring! Until you remember that it's not just food.

Last weekend all our family came home for Sunday dinner. They sat round the table, cheerful and chatty. The dog lay underneath it, ever hopeful. And as we passed round the plates, I thought, not for the first time, that food is more than eating.

It's like sharing all the things that go to make up a family. Warmth and flavour, good news and bad, giving and taking, part of each other and part of something bigger. Even washing up is more fun when everyone pitches in and does it together.

Primitive people used to share salt. I was reminded of this once when I was on an Indian reservation. Not that *they* were primitive—far from it.

We all met at the local Fried Chicken shop. We pulled the tables together and sat in a big circle. The local minister said grace, and we delved into the containers and doled out the food. And all at once it became a family party, Navajo Indians, Americans, and visiting British.

Eating together does strengthen the family ties.

'We are one family, as we share in the one loaf,' as the Christian communion service has it.

—Even when the 'loaf' is sausages!

We feast on the abundant food you provide;
You let us drink from the river of your goodness.
You are the source of all life.
Psalm 36:8

Heavenly Father, we thank you that you provide for all our needs. Help us to share with each other the good things of life.

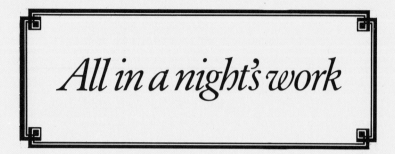

All in a night's work

IT was a first tooth, and our baby son was determined that the whole family should join in his triumph.

After six sleepless nights we were up, yet again. It was winter, and no central heating. However one wrapped up, it wasn't exactly fun to be pacing up and down, in slippered feet, rocking a howling baby.

We lived in the north of England, in a city where the houses clung to the steep hillsides, and the castle and cathedral towered on the topmost hills, with the valley and its river below.

We drew back the curtains to look out at the frosty night and the stars. There was no traffic and no noise to compete with the baby.

But to our surprise we were not alone—across the valley, in not a few homes, bedroom lights shone. Perhaps they were late-night revellers returning. Perhaps a miner or two on early shift, going out into the cold night. But more than likely they were young parents, like ourselves, thinking theirs was the only problem baby in the world.

I remember a young couple in our church taking their baby for a seaside holiday. And on the first night the howls of protest were so embarrassing that at dawn the father got up, dressed, put the baby in its push chair and set off for the pier.

He thought he was alone in the world—and met six other fathers, all in the same plight. They had quite a conversation, at the end of the pier, as the grey light turned to pink, and the sun came up.

And if a healthy baby can cause such mayhem, what about a sick one, or a baby born with handicap of mind or body? Then the feeling of being alone can become almost unbearable.

It seems impertinent to offer advice. I've only experienced such situations at second hand. And I've been astonished and humbled by the fortitude shown by such parents. They are a constant reminder to us that the ups and downs of family life are a sign that everything is quite normal.

So next time the baby gives you a sleepless night, try thanking God that the howls are proof of a good pair of lungs, and a healthy determination to make his presence felt.

And take a look out of the window for fellow sufferers —you are never alone!

Come unto me, all of you who are tired
from carrying heavy loads,
and I will give you rest.
Matthew 11:28

Dear God, sometimes we find family responsibility more than we can bear. In those moments, strengthen us. Help us to help each other, that our burden may turn to joy.

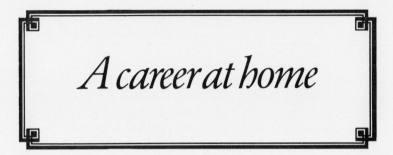

A career at home

IT was late in the evening. We'd had a meeting in the local school—a good meeting, cheerful and productive. People remarked on the good atmosphere.

Someone said, 'It's this hall—it's a very good school—the kids are happy here!'

There was some evidence of the day-time children: pictures on the wall, midget chairs and tables. And they did seem to have left a nice warm feeling in the place.

Then one man said that he'd been house-hunting recently, and one quite nice house had felt evil inside. Other people agreed. Houses, they said, took on the character of their owners. Well, I suppose it could be true. It made me think how important it is that our own homes should have a good 'feel'.

Someone has just written a book—very clever stuff and all that—proving that the most basic work in society is that done by women. Preparing food (and in the old days growing it too, for farming in primitive societies is usually done by women), cooking it, sewing clothes, cleaning. (I dare say even the very first housewives spent a fair bit of time keeping the cave clean!) And, most important of all, bearing and bringing up children.

So I'm not surprised women resent the implication in the phrase 'just a housewife'. What man when asked his job would say 'just an electrician', or 'just an advertising executive'?

For that matter, what woman who goes out to work

has to justify the importance of her job! Except perhaps to herself, which is a pity. We ought not to feel guilty about our careers.

But the career of motherhood and homemaking is beyond value and needs no justification. Its importance is incalculable and 'the rate for the job' is beyond assessment. Which of us can go on strike when the baby needs feeding?

It takes more energy, initiative, enthusiasm and commitment than almost any other job. And being a father is no picnic either. And it's all bound up with the 'feel' of the home.

Nowadays my role has changed a bit. Instead of sitting at home, looking after the children, we sit and wait for them to come home! But you can feel their presence around the house, however empty it is. And I hope the 'feel' is good!

The good wife 'is strong and respected
and not afraid of the future . . .
Charm is deceptive and beauty disappears,
but a woman who honours the Lord
should be praised.'
Proverbs 31:25, 30

Dear Father, make our homes places where you are known, where your Spirit is the air we breathe. May we find in you true joy and peace, through Jesus Christ our Lord.

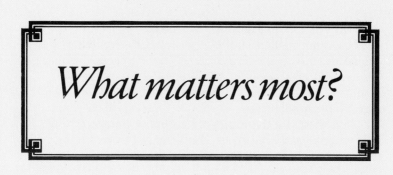

What matters most?

YOU know that game where they ask you what you'd grab first in the event of a fire? (I always say, 'My husband'!)

This summer, I came face to face with a couple who really had been faced with losing everything. In fact it wasn't a fire, it was a flood.

It happened one Easter weekend when they were expecting their four children home for a family get-together. The kitchen was full of food, and everything was perfect, except the weather. It had rained for days, and on the Saturday, word came through that the river was dangerously high.

That night, the water, dirty and contaminated, rose six feet inside their house. Furniture was ruined, possessions floated out into the street. Even their dog swam off and wasn't seen for a week.

'Did you lose everything?' we asked.

'No,' they replied, 'not everything. Oh, we lost all our "valuables". And the odd thing is, that if you'd asked us beforehand what we'd try to save, we'd have said the furniture, or the silver, or the television. But in fact, we didn't have much time.

'And these are the things we grabbed: photos of our kids when they were babies; this little gift from a holiday we had; our wedding photos, and some old books we loved. None of them is valuable, really. But to us they're priceless.

'And we learnt something important. Belongings don't really matter. We can start again; the chairs and tables and carpets can be replaced.

'What we discovered above all, were our friends. Even people we'd never seen before came to help us clean up. And our children worked like anything and never complained.

'Now we talk about before and after the flood! And we don't want to go back to the old ways. Our nightmare has turned into a beautiful new beginning.

'It made us wonder what's the most important part of our home. The furniture? Or the people in it?'

I know what I'd choose.

> *Jesus said . . . a person's true life*
> *is not made up of the things he owns,*
> *no matter how rich he may be.*
> Luke 12:15
>
> Dear Lord, help us to recognize those things
> in life that are worthwhile, and cling to
> them. Whatever the future may hold for us,
> may we put our trust in you.

Pretty poor company

I GO to this weekly art class. There are about twenty of us—and most of us work in the day time. The men have long journeys home from work and sometimes rush in at the last moment.

Most of the women just sit there for the first few minutes, collecting their thoughts. Some, if they've been alone all day, talk madly to the first person they meet.

Some days I don't feel like going at all. Then I remember one woman who came last year. Each Monday evening she would sit there producing very fine delicate drawings. She was very reserved, not shy exactly, but self-contained.

Once I made some remark about feeling very tired and not wanting to make the effort.

'Oh, but you must,' she exclaimed, and went on to tell us that for years she'd been tied at home. Their son was mentally handicapped and in need of constant attention. At last her husband had a job where he could get home in time to take over, and she could go out for an evening.

She said it was like a new lease of life. We all felt rather ashamed.

I know it's different when the children are young, and they keep your hands full all day. Your brain just seems to stop working. It's not everyone who can be excited by nappies and baby talk for hours on end.

You miss adult conversation. You even miss the in-tray, or the journey to work, or the phone going all the time. So you do need a regular 'out'. You need a class to go to, a shopping spree all on your own, or a friend to go out with. And your husband ought to take over the kids on a regular basis and push you out of the door.

If the state can't run enough nursery schools, there should be more self-help amongst young mothers to run their own groups. The churches, too, need to give all the help they can to keep young parents sane.

Meanwhile the lifelines are there, even though we don't always listen. There are interests we can keep up, however modestly. Radio can be an enormous help, the TV is a window on the world.

I used to read while feeding the baby. I have a friend who keeps a missionary prayer list and a map of the world over the kitchen sink.

To meet all the demands of a growing family, we need to grow as persons, so we can't afford to let ourselves go! Cabbages are fine for eating, but they make pretty poor company!

For everything there is a season:
and a time for every matter under heaven.
Ecclesiastes 3:1

Lord, help us not to be burdened by too much care. Help us to take delight in the work of our hands and the opportunities to grow that each day brings. And help us to make time for you.

Potter's clay

MY grandfather was a master potter. In his day you served a seven-year apprenticeship, and the work was long and hard. In the early days he made everyday dishes and the sort of flower-pots gardeners use. But he became very skilled and some of his work is still

around—beautifully shaped vases and decorated plaques.

It's said in the family that he was a bit wild as a young man, but later he was converted by a Baptist mission. He loved reading his Bible, and when he talked it was hard to tell where his words left off and the Bible began. I used to love listening to his stories.

When I knew him, he was retired, but he had his own potter's wheel. We used to watch him plonk the wet clay on it, and turn the wheel with a foot pedal until the clay spun round under his hands. The index finger of his right hand was distinctly curved, from years of pressing it against the inside of the pots.

He loved his grandchildren and made each of the girls a tiny dolls' tea service, each piece hand-painted and decorated.

I always think of my grandfather when I read Jeremiah's words:

> *So I went down to the potter's house*
> *and saw the potter working at his wheel.*
> *Whenever a piece of pottery turned out imperfect,*
> *he would take the clay*
> *and make it into something else.*
> *Then the Lord said to me . . .*
> *You are in my hands*
> *just like the clay in the potter's hands.*
> Jeremiah 18:1-6

We are all like clay that can be fashioned for good or ill. Help us, Father, to be sensitive to your will. We want our lives to be shaped by you, to bear the mark of your hand.

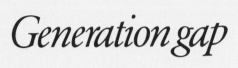

Generation gap

I ONCE spent an evening a week working with some women in prison. They were all young girls, hardly out of their teens, and full of bright talk and plausible excuses. Nearly all of them came from broken homes and, under the tough exterior, there was often bitterness and loneliness.

One evening, after the class, one of the girls got permission to take me downstairs to see her baby. She was still feeding it, so it lived in the prison nursery and was taken for walks in the prison grounds.

I stood at the end of the cot looking at it. All small babies turn your heart over, but this one doubly so. I thought—what a start to life! What grim surroundings and gloomy prospects.

I was then expecting our third child, and I lost touch with the girls. But I heard soon after that that young mother had absconded with her child. I was not surprised.

It seems a long way from our comfortable family circles. But we all face problems in bringing up a family, and sometimes we fear that our kids could go wrong. After all, we think, it happened to so-and-so.

And anyway our kids see grown-ups who are 'on the make', who grab everything for themselves, who deal dishonestly, who drink too much, eat too much, take too many tranquillizers.

Or maybe they just look at their respectable parents who seem to put jobs, or ambition, or money, or the house before everything else. And they think, that's not for us.

So before we start a League for Battered Parents, let's remember that a lot of young people are reacting against a way of life that isn't very worthwhile. And although they may not be very clear about what they want, their rejection of our world has some very healthy motives.

There have always been 'generation gaps', but they don't have to end in constant rows, or total silence. We can keep up a dialogue, however uncertain.

If our children's despair expresses itself in a drink problem or a drugs problem, we've really got a 'person' problem—and people need people.

We don't have to agree, but we do have to keep talking, and listening. And we have to look at our own position to see whether we've got it right, or wrong. For if there is some good in our way of life, our young people may eventually 'come to themselves', and find their way back to our homes.

At last he came to his senses and said . . .
'I will get up and go to my father . . .
He was still a long way from home
when his father saw him;
his heart was filled with pity,
and he ran, threw his arms round his son,
and kissed him.
Luke 15:17 (the lost son)

Dear Father God, help us to keep a welcome in our hearts for all young ones who are part of our life—no matter what they may have done. Give us a forgiving heart, a sympathetic ear and a readiness to share in their concerns. Make us aware of our own weaknesses, and keep us from pride.

Guide-lines

W E'VE a new arrival in our house!' I informed my
neighbour. And then added hurriedly, lest she
think we'd got the pram out again: 'It's a yard
long, and yesterday it ate my shoes. At least it ate the left
one, so the right shoe isn't much use now.'

'Is it a goat?' she asked suspiciously.

'No,' I laughed. 'It may be a yard long but it's only a
foot tall. It's a sort of dachshund. And it hasn't half made a
difference to our lives.'

Well, so it had. For a start we had to learn to shut our
gate. And where the garden fence had a hole in it, we put
some chicken wire. Of course, at first he crept under and
went in search of his real mum. And because the grass was
so tall, and he so near the ground, we had a job to find him
in the neighbours' gardens. But after a few weeks he
seemed to adopt us as a family.

He was scared of the park at first. He would go slowly
toward the gates, and cringe at the sight of big dogs. And
on the way home he'd wag his tail and hurry.

Then we discovered that he liked being on the lead. We
thought it was because he felt that it was *we* who were on
the lead—he had us safely in tow. Little did he know!

In an amazingly short time we all settled into a routine.
Of course, we had a few mishaps but it was all part of the
growing-up process. We cuffed him off the best furniture.
He nudged us out of our chairs when it was time for walks.

We fed him, and he rewarded us with joyous yelps and tail-wagging.

The point is, there had to be adjustments on both sides. The limits had to be laid down. Both we and the dog needed to know the boundaries.

I once knew some parents who fervently believed that on no account must they say 'No!' to their little son. They said they wanted him to grow up without fear.

Before he was three, he'd fallen off a shed and broken all his front teeth. And his mother nearly had a nervous breakdown.

We know that life involves risk, but we all need to know the sensible limits. Our children need guide-lines. Freedom isn't flying off in all directions at once. It's learning to deal with the risks, to change what can be changed, to accept what can't, to fit in with other people, to be the best that we can be. With a little help from our friends. And a lot of help from God.

You will show me the path that leads to life;
your presence fills me with joy.
Psalm 16:11

Dear God, we have so much to learn. Keep us from pride. We depend on you to set the boundaries of our life and to surround us with your loving care.

'All kinds of everything'

DO you remember a simple little song called 'All kinds of everything'? It was rather a nice song, a sort of celebration of all the little things that make up the many-splendoured thing that love is.

It's made up of nappies and cots, of first steps and stumbles, of school and homework, of laughter and tears.

I was turning out a cupboard yesterday and I found a Christmas card made by one of the children. There have been many Christmases, and birthdays, and such-like. And how many presents have changed hands?

Sometimes I think we give presents because love is so big a thing, it's almost embarrassing. So, instead of saying, 'I love you', we wrap something up, put a label on it, pretend it's something we need.

And surely one of the really great presents changes hands on our wedding day. The ring is slipped on our finger, as though to say, 'We are ringed around, tied together, part of one circle.' We can't put it into words, so we make the gesture instead.

When I was a kid, we didn't have the money to buy flowers for Mothering Sunday. We used to go out into the meadows and pick wild flowers. Those meadows are part of a housing estate now. You can't get something for nothing—even with effort—any more.

And giving presents has become a chore, shopping in supermarkets and big stores. But when the gift is handed over, you forget all that. Because the gift is just a cover-up—a way of saying, 'You mean all kinds of everything' to me!'

So, when God wanted to show us his love, he gave us the best gift of all, wrapped up in swaddling bands, and labelled 'Jesus'.

For God loved the world so much
that he gave his only Son . . .
John 3:16

Dear God, you have given us so much. Help us to love one another as truly and deeply as you would have us love. Help us never to be ashamed of our feelings. And make us sensitive to the feelings of others.

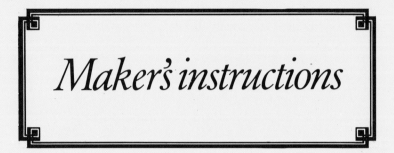

Maker's instructions

WE met a farmer in the Mid-West of America. He told us he was running his farm by himself with the help of machinery. When he was a boy, he said, the same land would have given work to a whole village full of people.

Our countryside is full of machines nowadays. We have a friend who grows potatoes. He always says that no tool is as good as the human hand—or as complicated. Although he uses a machine to harvest his fields, lots of good potatoes get left in the ground.

I walked behind the machine once, and filled up a sack with big pink-skinned potatoes. Delicious! But a back-breaking business if you had to do it all day.

Do you ever buy potatoes, ready washed, in plastic bags? You should see the machine that organizes that. It's like a very long car-wash. The potatoes are taken up by wooden rollers, sorted into sizes, sprayed with water, and finally dried with warm air before being packed.

'Does it ever go wrong?' I asked.

'Yes,' the manager admitted ruefully. 'Last week it got too hot. The potatoes all came out roasted.'

We all know the feeling. The washing-machine that packs up just as you've put in the biggest load ever. I remember my neighbour getting a tartan rug caught in a spin dryer. We ended up with rainbow-coloured threads all over the kitchen.

Sometimes you can mend the machine yourself or get

someone to do it quickly. But if it's something really big, you send it back to the maker. He's the only one who knows how the machine works, and has the spare parts to mend it.

Why don't we remember that when it comes to people? God made us. He really knows what's good for us, and how people work best. And if something goes wrong with our lives, he can help us to put it right. He is the real expert.

And we could carry this idea further and say that we need regular servicing! Keeping in touch with him by saying our prayers and reading his word, and worshipping him are all part of the service we need.

It's not what we do for him, but what he can do for us that's so marvellous.

You, Lord, are all I have,
and you give me all I need;
my future is in your hands.
Psalm 16:5

O God, you know us so much better than we can know ourselves. 'Examine me, O God, and know my mind; test me and discover my thoughts . . . And guide me in the everlasting way.'

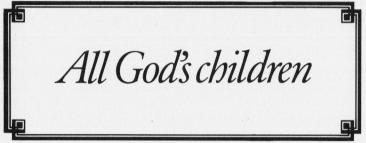

All God's children

IN my teens I belonged to a church youth club. There were lots of things to do—talks and discussions and games. We were a cheerful lot, always on the go, never still. And one of the most popular activities was square dancing.

Only one person never took part. He couldn't. No fancy wheelchairs in those days.

Frank was a polio victim.

His arms and shoulders were very powerful, but his wizened, shrunken legs were supported by irons and he walked with two sticks.

But he was an extraordinary person. I never heard him complain. He was full of concern for people, interested in everything that went on. Nothing passed him by.

In fact, he ran the church magazine, churning out hundreds of copies on an old duplicator. Especially, he always had time for the kids in the youth club, and people told him all sorts of personal things—things that never got into the magazine!

When he died, aged thirty, they hung his two sticks in the church, in the shape of a cross. His pain and his crippled limbs had been a cross, but he'd used them for so much good. Afterwards we told each other that we'd never noticed his handicap. To us he was a complete person. He was whole.

I don't think God looks at people as we do. When a baby is born we ask, 'Is he perfect?' We mean, has he got all his fingers and toes? We think of height and weight and brown hair and bright eyes.

But none of us is perfect. Some are more out of true than others. But the better you know a person, the less you notice what they look like. You begin to see them, as it were, from the inside—as God does.

The other day, I discovered that the words 'whole' and 'holy' both come from an old word meaning 'complete'. So I suppose we felt that Frank was a 'holy' person.

He certainly made the world a better, brighter place. He was one of God's special people. And I'm glad I knew him.

Who would have believed what we now report?
Who could have seen the Lord's hand in this? . . .
After a life of suffering,
he will again have joy;
he will know that he did not suffer in vain!
Isaiah 53 (the suffering 'servant' here
is usually identified with Jesus himself)

Dear God, we do not understand suffering—we only know that you are in it with us. Teach us to discover your presence in the bad times as well as the good. We put our trust in your love.

The pink geranium

M Y neighbour delivers hot meals to elderly people. One day she came home with more than she'd taken out—a huge pink geranium in a pot. An old lady had grown the flower with loving care, and it was her 'thank you' for all the help she'd received.

But I suspect it was more than that. Perhaps my neighbour was her only contact with the outside world. The old lady had once been a busy citizen, but she never went out any more.

Her friends had all moved away, or died. She'd no family. And she was tired of eating alone—she wanted to be part of a bigger feast, of the life beyond her four walls.

Sometimes we take the children from our church to the local old people's home. At the time, no one wants to go. It's a bit of a nuisance, giving up a Sunday afternoon. We sing hymns, and tell a story and the children play some music. You're not always sure that anyone's listening!

Then you go round and talk to them, and all sorts of scraps of information come out. This one has been abroad half her life, that one was an important business man. Sometimes they will paint a picture of life as it was almost a century ago.

As we go out and gather in the car park, no one says, 'Well that's over, thank goodness.' Because in fact we have enjoyed the hour spent there. Instead of our helping the old people, they have blessed us. And not least by reminding us that *we* can go out freely into the sunshine.

It's worth teaching your children to talk to old folk.
You can start by doing it yourself. I know it can be
difficult, especially when they want to tell us how to
behave! But mostly it's very rewarding. And often a special
bond develops between the very young and the very old.

Besides, they have all the time in the world to listen,
and that's worth a lot! Even more than a pink geranium.

> *You have taught me ever since I was young,*
> *and I still tell of your wonderful acts.*
> *Now that I am old and my hair is grey,*
> *do not abandon me, O God!*
> Psalm 71:17

Dear Lord, keep us from being impatient
with those who are old or lonelier than we
are. Teach us to listen with sympathy and
act with kindness. Above all, help us to be
thankful for the countless people who
enrich our own lives and encourage us.

Partnership

I WAS off work with a sore throat. I had chosen a good day to be ill! After weeks of cold, wet weather, the spring sun had at last broken through.

I sat at a window overlooking the garden, and watched the straggling snowdrops and crocuses lift their faces to the sun. The hedge was tinged with green, and beneath it the daffodils were pushing up, buds still closed, but a promise of new life to come.

Two blackbirds were nest-building. They took such care selecting a site. They examined closely every bush in the garden, flying in and out, and poking about. Then, apparently making up their minds and reaching a decision, they both started systematically searching the borders for bits of grass and twigs, flying to and fro with great energy and dedication. A real partnership of effort.

I had the newspaper to read, and as I glanced at it my peace was shattered. Apart from the usual gloom on the front page, a headline inside caught my eye.

'Man sentenced to five years in prison' for 'hurling baby across room like a football'.

Now I'm not a person to explode into self-righteous horror when I read about something like that. I know only too well the despair one can feel after nights of sleepless torment, when a baby's shrill demands can eat into one's very brain.

I remember, one night, walking the bedroom floor for the umpteenth time, suddenly shaking my screaming offspring. I was at the end of my tether with his constant crying. But fortunately my husband woke up and took him over.

At such a time the partnership of marriage makes real sense. Bringing up a family is a strain on anyone's capabilities, and we need to recognize our dependence on each other.

So it doesn't do to sit in judgement on others. But it does suggest that we ought to be on the look-out for people under stress. The whole Christian family, in particular, ought to offer all the loving concern it can to young parents, and even more especially to single parents who struggle alone.

So let's treasure the partnerships we already have, and do our best to extend them to others.

Don't worry about anything,
but in all your prayers ask God for what you need
. . . And God's peace,
which is far beyond human understanding
will keep your hearts and minds safe
in union with Christ Jesus.
Philippians 4:6-7

Dear Father God, no matter how often we disappoint you, you never let us go. Always your loving arms are there to guide us and support us. Help us to trust each other. As our love grows, may òthers be blessed through us.

A death in the family

I WAS taken to see my grandmother, who was dying.
Her big old-fashioned bed had been brought down to
the front room to make constant attendance on her
possible. She lay propped up on white pillows, her face
and hair a perfect match for them. She knew no one.

It was almost a year to the day since my grandfather
had died, and I remembered my grandmother following his
coffin up the familiar church aisle. Someone had placed a
bunch of pansies in her hand, and she was quite unaware
of the folk around her.

It had been a long partnership, and once broken she
had no further use for her life. A few days after my visit,
they were reunited. It seemed right and fitting, and I
couldn't feel sad as I had felt sad at the death of my
grandpa.

In our bright new modern world we have pushed such experiences out of our homes. Few babies are born in the family bed—few old people die there.

In many ways it's a blessing. Childbirth is safer, and fewer old people end their days in pain and distress. Families don't feel the strain. Everything is catered for, from the cradle to the grave. But have we lost something in the process?

I think we have. When my own mother died, my children were quite young. We didn't take them to the funeral, we thought they were too young to understand. We were quite wrong. Years later our daughter expressed regret that she had been left out in this way.

We all need to share the sense of loss, the natural mourning that such occasions bring. And we need to talk about the person who has died, not shy away from the hurt.

A death in the hospital can seem very unreal to the rest of the family, and the reality of it needs to be brought home. Home is where grief belongs as well as joy.

And in a home lit by God, things eventually fall into place, and both life and death take on new meaning.

For I am certain that nothing can separate us
from his love: neither death nor life . . .
there is nothing in all creation that will
ever be able to separate us from the love of God
which is ours through Christ Jesus our Lord.
Romans 8:38-39

Dear God, we thank you for all those whose lives have shown forth your presence. Give us the help we need to be faithful to you to our life's end.

The things we do!

IT'S amazing what we do for our children!
My neighbour was telling me, once, how her mother had loathed mice. But she gave way in the end and allowed her daughter to keep a pet mouse. Providing it stayed in the shed.

And so it did, until one day her mother went into the shed and found the cage door open. Overcoming her natural impulse to flee the place, she searched high and low for the missing mouse, knowing how upset the child would be.

At last she spotted it hiding in a corner, and before she could think, her hand flew out and caught the tiny tail. She carefully replaced the mouse in the cage and shut the door.

Only then did she discover, hiding under an overturned food container, the original inhabitant!

She'd found a second mouse, who wasn't lost. My friend's mother, over-jealous of her child's happiness, had caught a stray field-mouse, and doubled her assets.

The things we do! Even I have been known to place worms on hooks for eager little fishermen. But I draw the line at mice.

Guinea-pigs, now, are a different matter. The first one we bought was of such an innocent and youthful appearance that we were totally unprepared for the impending event. We even accused our children of grossly over-feeding her.

Then one Saturday morning she had three offspring. They appeared like a minor miracle, and within half an hour were washed and fluffed up, as pretty as could be, and feeding almost immediately on a mixed diet!

Our children, who had witnessed this birth and transformation, were entranced. And a very good thing too. There's a lot to be said for discovering that life is not only natural but beautiful as well.

So let's look at things with our children. Things that are child-sized. Daisies, and ducks on the pond, all the colours and patterns and little details that we grown-ups get used to, and pass without noticing.

It's not so much what we do for our children, as what they do for us! They help us see the world through a child's eyes.

Lord, you have made so many things!
How wisely you have made them all!
The earth is filled with your creatures.
Psalm 104:24

Creator God, give us eyes wide open to the wonders of your world. May its infinite variety speak to us of your greatness and love. May we take delight in simple things, seeing in them the perfection of your infinite life.

No end of time

CHILDREN can be infuriating, and one of their worst faults is a complete lack of any sense of time. They simply don't understand that there are only twenty-four hours in a day! And that you simply haven't got the time to linger by the toy counter when there's all the shopping to be done, or to play hopscotch on the path when you've the beds to make and the washing to deal with.

And what happens when you're in a hurry—and you have to be at the school gates at 3 o'clock, or else? The more you hurry, the slower they get. There's no end to the time it can take to put on a pair of shoes or tie a lace.

And I've known my youngest, placed in front of a basin of hot water, with soap, and told to wash, to be found half an hour later, gazing at a basin of perfectly clean, cold water, still unwashed. What was he thinking, all that time?

In vain the rest of the family would cry, 'But you want to go out, don't you?' He did, but he didn't want to be hurried.

For grown-ups, time is money, and we daren't waste a second.

But now that the children are older, what do I remember, looking back? Beds made, and shopping done? Housework finished and work carried out efficiently? Not a bit of it.

I remember the odd unexpected moments, when

suddenly and stealthily, eternity broke into our human time.

Moments spent by the paddling-pool, instead of hurrying home from school; visits to the local park to see the black sheep with curly horns, kept for city children to enjoy. I even remember whole chunks out of books read so often that the kids knew if I tried to skip a page or two.

Time is important. We can't live without regular food and reasonable surroundings. But there are much more important things than efficiency, as all children know instinctively. And 'to stand and stare' is not necessarily a waste of time.

So next time your kid tugs you by the sleeve, don't be in such a hurry. Take a look, or lend an ear. Of such things are the Kingdom of Heaven!

Look at the birds . . . they do not sow seeds,
gather a harvest and put it in barns;
yet your Father in heaven takes care of them!
Aren't you worth more than birds? . . .
So do not worry about tomorrow . . .
Matthew 6:26, 34

Dear Lord, we are so full of care that we are careless about you. Teach us to use time wisely. Help us not to be so anxious about the future that we neglect the present.

Mummy doesn't love you?

I WAS waiting outside the nursery for my youngest son. Clean little girls in cotton frocks, nice little boys in T-shirts and shorts, all tumbled through the door, laughing and shouting.

Then out came our red-faced, tousled scamp, sleeves rolled up, thumping his neighbours for all he was worth. They didn't look much better!

'No!' I yelled, catching him by the scruff of his torn shirt. 'You're not to hit people!'

Sudden silence.

'But Mum,' wailed my offspring, 'they're my friends!'

Honestly, what can you do with them?

But of course, in a sense, he was right. If you can't fight your friends, who can you fight? And this sort of friendly battle has no malice in it.

But what about those rages that possess small children, like sudden storms of thunder and lightning.

'I hate you,' shouts the small child, face red and fists flailing. It may be frustration, it may be pure anger at not getting what he wants.

There's one golden rule. I haven't always kept it, but I know it's true. You must *never* say, 'Don't do that or Mummy (Daddy) won't love you.'

For one thing it's not true. However outrageous your child's behaviour, you may stop liking him, but you won't cease to love.

You'll want him to change, to understand, to grow up.

But always your love must be a constant in his life, as
God's love is in ours, no matter how bad we are.
  And try to take these small storms lightly.
  'Never mind. Come and give us a kiss!'
In the end, he'll want to do just that.

> *I know that your goodness and love*
> *will be with me all my life;*
> *and your house will be my home as long as I live.*
> Psalm 23:6
>
> Dear Father God, help us to be worthy of
> the children you've placed in our care.
> Freely you have loved us; may we give our
> love freely too.

43

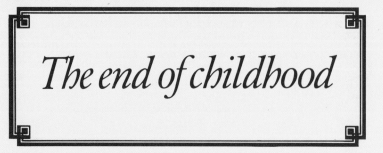

The end of childhood

OUR son is growing up now. We went to see him in a play last week. It was a powerful play and it began with strong, ugly words. It was strange to hear such alien speech from him—he's not usually given to bad language, at least in our presence!

But the real obscenity was in the situation portrayed by the play—the reactions of family and friends to a handicapped boy. It was played out in such a way that it hurt the audience. It was meant to, and that was good.

We must not, indeed we cannot, shield our children from the bad and the ugly. When they are young we try to keep them from danger, moral as well as physical. But as they grow up, they need to face facts. And one fact is that there is much in the world that is tawdry, and even more that is downright evil.

So how do we meet it?

I suppose the first essential is to keep our lines of communication open. A family can't exist in silence. Feelings need to be expressed, opinions stated.

The most united family I ever knew used, when the children were young, to conduct most of their business in shouts. I found it quite daunting at first, but soon learned that under this extraordinary and boisterous behaviour there were real relationships.

And the second essential is tolerance. We mustn't expect our children always to agree with us. We have our ways and they don't want to be carbon copies. But they do

want us to be firm, to know our own minds. We mustn't be rigid, but it's far worse to be jellyfish, floating about in a sea of doubt.

Jesus said that evil does not come from the outside, but from within. And if our inner lives are strong in Christ, evil can trouble but not overcome us.

The morning after the play, we asked our son what he would like to do.

'Go to the zoo,' was the unexpected reply. He'd not been to that particular zoo since he was six years old, and it was a strange pleasure to cover the ground once more, noticing the newcomers, recognizing the old. And instead of us showing him, he was pointing things out to us.

It's good when they grow up!

> *. . . things we have heard and known,*
> *things that our fathers told us.*
> *We will not keep them from our children;*
> *We will tell the next generation*
> *about the Lord's power and his great deeds*
> *and the wonderful things he has done.*
> *Psalm 78:3-4*

Lord God, give us the strength to speak out against evil and not to be afraid to let others know where we stand. Teach us the true meaning of goodness.

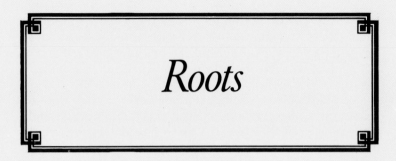

Roots

I HAVE had a number of formidable elderly aunts. Well, I suppose they weren't always elderly, but they lived to such a great age that they seemed to be elderly for a very long time.

One of them was convinced that the stories of people going to the moon were all part of an elaborate hoax, and no amount of television reporting or newspaper articles would persuade her to think differently. She died, happily secure in her belief that the world was exactly as it was when she was a girl.

Another of my aunts, however, took a brisk interest in all that went on. Up to the age of ninety she acted as a repository for all the messages that came from far-flung members of the family, passing on news from one person to another as they visited her.

We miss her sadly. People today are so busy that they don't write letters, or talk to the neighbours, or keep in touch with relatives, as they did when I was a child.

I think children need this sense of belonging, of having roots, of ties with the past.

One of my aunts looked after an old lady who was cripped with arthritis. We used to visit her. She was like a tiny bright-eyed bird, propped up in her bed and surrounded by white pillows edged with lace. Her hands, claw-like, would smooth the sheets and invite us to sit nearby. Then she would tell us stories of her past.

As a girl she had been house-maid to Charles Kingsley,

who wrote *The Water Babies*. It's hard to believe that one could talk to someone whose memories took her back to boy chimney-sweeps. I remember, too, how she kept a bottle of boiled sweets by the bed, and popped one in our mouths before we left.

Young people go through a phase when all they want to hear about is the latest craze. Fashion changes weekly, and the gap between them and the past seems to widen every moment.

But don't be deceived. They are only 'putting on the style'. Underneath, they are as unsure of themselves as youngsters ever were. They need the sense of continuity, the bonds that hold communities together.

History is more than dates in a book. It's our link to reality.

Another thing I remember about my aunts is that they all went to church. They were Sunday school teachers, and supported the missionaries, and went to meetings, and visited the sick. The church was the focal point of their lives, and their Christian faith was the vital link that held everything together.

We usually have a family get-together at Christmas. We miss the familiar faces of the aunts. But wouldn't they be proud to see the family, still at it!

With our own ears we have heard it, O God
—our ancestors have told us about it,
about the great things you did in their time,
in the days of long ago.
Psalm 44:1

Dear God, you who are the same yesterday, today and for ever, we praise you for your guidance in past years. We give thanks for the relationships that have moulded us. In your mercy, make our lives meaningful too.

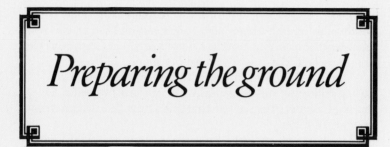

Preparing the ground

IT may seem irreverent to start this by writing about the death of a dog. But when our first dachshund was killed on the road, the whole family grieved bitterly. It was a sudden, violent end, and we were unprepared for it. Gradually the loss came home to us, and many tears were shed.

More often, death comes in slower, even harsher ways. It is very hard for grown-ups to accept changes in the ones they love. Long illness can bring about deterioration in minds and personalities and alter physical appearance almost beyond recognition.

This is even harder for children to accept. They are still unsure of their own identity, still working out their lives. And to see a close relative seriously ill is often a traumatic experience.

When my mother-in-law was in a coma, about a week

or so before she died, we took our teenage son to see her. We thought we had been wrong in keeping the family from such experiences. But now we were not sure. Certainly, the next day, he did not want to see her again.

A beloved grandmother, who had so enjoyed her 'young folk', yet now was unaware of their presence. Or was she? Sometimes we felt that she knew that loved ones were around her.

And what of our son? I remember how shocked I was, when as a young girl I saw a dead person. The image remained with me for years. But that may not of itself be a bad thing.

Many experiences come to us before we are old enough to understand. Love is one of them. We realise it gradually, sometimes when it is too late. But we always benefit from it.

And things that happen in a loving context can be assimilated unconsciously. Years later, when we meet a similar loss, the ground has been prepared. Loss is an inevitable part of life and, when accepted, it can indeed bear fruit.

> Jesus said, 'The hour has now come
> for the Son of Man to receive great glory.
> I am telling you the truth:
> a grain of wheat remains no more than a single grain
> unless it is dropped into the ground and dies.
> If it does die, then it produces many grains.
> Whoever loves his own life will lose it.'
> John 12:23-25

Dear God, none of us can escape death. Help us so to know Jesus as our Lord and Saviour that we may no longer fear death. May we think of death as the gateway to eternal life.

Where do we stand?

S HE stood there in the dock, in a flowery dress and a picture hat—all sweetness and light. We'd sat through four or five dreary cases, and this one was comic relief.

She'd been caught, at midnight, hopping over the fence of a law-abiding citizen, and stealing a rose. Well, several, actually. And it turned out that she made a habit of it, cycling round the town late at night, pinching roses.

Why? Because she had a rather dismal room, and she liked flowers.

The magistrate tried to look stern. The laughter rippled round the court-room. Even the police wore broad grins. She was let off with a caution. Maybe if she'd been a gipsy the outcome would have been different. In fact, she was a student.

The same week, I'd been shopping in a big department store. It was fairly early and not very crowded. There was a sudden sharp clattering of heels. A woman and a young girl were running down the stairs, with a store detective in hot pursuit. I caught a glimpse of white frightened faces as the shoplifters ran past.

I don't know what their excuse was, but I do know that stealing in our society has moved a long way from pinching apples for fun, or a loaf of bread out of sheer need. A lot of people think they can take what they like, at anyone's expense. And children soon get the message.

So maybe for their sake and our own we have to make

the other side very plain. We can start with the words. Taking what you want, regardless, is not 'borrowing', or 'winning', it is stealing. Let's call it that. A Christian has to take a stand somewhere. And then remember that we all pay for it in the end.

> *We know that we belong to God*
> *even though the whole world*
> *is under the rule of the Evil One.*
> 1 John 5:19

Father, you set us a high standard. We belong to you. Help us to stand up for what is right, not only in our words, but in our deeds.

Growing up

THERE was a time when marriage was the only escape for a woman—a chance to leave her parents' home and start a new life. A chance to be a recognized adult, even though her husband made most of the decisions. (Or did he? When I think of some of my elderly aunts, with their energy and determination, I have a feeling they had a thing or two to say about the way things were run!)

Still, the situation is a bit different today. Marriage certainly isn't the only option, and for some young people it doesn't even seem to be an attractive one.

I must say, marriage came as a bit of a shock to me. For one thing, I'd had a busy job and liked it. I shared a flat with a couple of other girls. We had plenty of friends and went out a lot—nothing very smart, but it was fun. And if I wanted an evening in, I could please myself.

When my special boyfriend was around we went everywhere together. And then for weeks on end he'd be away.

In my day, you didn't get married while you were still a student. But even that had advantages. Privacy, for one thing. Time to put your curlers in, or read a book; time to think. Not too much pressure. Time to grow up.

Growing up in the 1980s is much harder. Kids may seem free—but they have to set all their own limits. And without much experience to fall back on. Don't be taken in by confident looks! They are as scared as we were, sometimes.

What can a Mum do to help? Don't laugh at them, for a start. And if you nag them (and we all do), try explaining that it's because you worry about them, because you care.

Open your door to their friends, however freaky, but don't let them take advantage of you. They don't *have* to take the place apart. And they can wash up as well as you can.

Discuss money with them. (It's amazing how secretive some parents are about their income.) But don't keep throwing expense at them. After all, they didn't choose to be born.

Support them with love and understanding. That's of more value than money.

And you can't watch over them all the time, so trust them. If your home has genuinely been a place of love, and the openness which love makes possible, one day theirs will be, too.

> *If any of you lacks wisdom, he should pray*
> *to God, who will give it to him; because God gives*
> *generously and graciously to all.*
> James 1:5
>
> Dear God, you alone give wisdom and understanding. Help us so to surround our loved ones with the knowledge of you that their feet may be led into the way of life.

Keeping in touch

SOMETIMES we make innocent remarks that cut other people to the quick. It's not that we mean to hurt. It's just lack of thought or sensitivity.

The woman in front of me was filling in a form—family details. At the space for 'number of children', she hesitated. I laughed, thinking of my own idiocy when it comes to forms.

'You can't remember,' I joked.

Silence. Then a halting explanation. She'd had four children, but two of them had died in their late teens— suicides. She said it was manic depression due to inherited chemical imbalance. Her youngest child was just coming up to the age when the dreadful condition might reveal itself.

As she unfolded the awful sequence of events, her own manner was quiet, gentle, almost apologetic. She didn't want to upset me!

It was an hour later, after much talk, that I asked her how she managed to keep her own life intact.

'Meditation,' she replied. She didn't mean anything strange or technical. But every day, before getting her husband's breakfast and then herself going to work, she would spend an hour turning her heart and mind towards God. Sometimes she would just sit in the window and look at her garden—really look—allow it to speak of a loving Creator.

She admitted that it had been very hard at first. All

sorts of angry thoughts and resentments had filled her mind. Gradually she had come to accept all that had happened. She didn't understand it, but she believed that God was with her in the pain, and that one day she would understand. Most important, she had persisted in her prayers, making time to be still, with God.

We all look at our children and wonder about the future. Will they grow up strong and good? Will they be successful? Will they be happy? What kind of world will be theirs in a decade or two?

We can make some provision. Give them a good start. Help them to choose wisely. Surround them with things that are 'lovely and of good report'. But we are not in control.

God is. And we need to keep in touch with him. So, however busy our lives, we need some quiet moments. Moments to sense, behind the immediate world, the reality on which we all ultimately depend.

> *God is our refuge and strength,*
> *a very present help in trouble . . .*
> *'Be still and know that I am God.'*
> Psalm 46:1, 10
>
> Lord God, so fill our hearts and minds with your presence that all fear and resentment is driven out. You are our refuge and you give us the strength we need.

Honestly?

OUR local newspaper carried a front page spread this
week on a group of kids who've been terrorizing
the neighbourhood, snatching old ladies' handbags
and the like. It referred to 'thoughtless' youngsters.

I fell to wondering what our grandparents would have
called them! 'Thieving little devils' perhaps? And the term
devil would have carried some deep meaning. The devil, or
evil, would have been seen in the violence and the stealing.

And no one would have been in doubt about what
would happen if they were caught. Most kids would see the
justice of that.

Nevertheless there must be very few families where the
problem of honesty never crops up. Often parents are
ashamed to admit it. But take the initiative, raise the
questions, and a flood of comment is often the result.

Nearly all young children go through a phase of taking
things. Sometimes they don't even 'want' what they take
but leave it lying around in the most obvious way. It's
difficult to argue at this stage. After all, they collect
everything, pebbles and pins, bits of paper, sweets, often
unmentionable debris.

To them it's a secret fascinating extension of
themselves, so don't throw away their rubbish. It may be
more important than we know. (I once threw away an
unspeakably dirty teddy bear, only to be reminded of this
awful mistake years later by a reproachful daughter.)

Young children find it difficult to share things. Perhaps

they need really to establish a sense of possession, before they can take the risk of sharing. And perhaps they will not know how to respect other people's property until they are sure about having some of their own.

When it comes to older children, I think plain speaking and honest dealing are the order of the day.

It's not easy to live up to this all the time, but if we are too greedy, too bothered about appearances, if we think that success is more important than satisfaction, money than effort, we mustn't be surprised if our kids think everything has a price tag, and easy pickings are better than hard work.

But they have to learn that if you take what you want, you pay for it sooner or later.

Above all, we need to talk about these things. If our way of life is worth offering to our children, then it's worth making the effort to spell it out. We may even find that they have something to teach us about being honest, in return.

You must shine among them
like stars lighting up the sky,
as you offer them the message of life.
Philippians 2:15

O Lord, we often fail in our efforts to be a beacon in a dark world. Give us your pure light, so that we may reflect your love in our lives, and so help to point the way to you.

Safe and sound

I HAVE some friends who have a particularly lively four-year-old. His mother says he's very obedient. She only has to tell him to stop doing something and he immediately obeys—only to be found five minutes later doing something even worse!

Most young children are infinitely curious, and endlessly inventive, always up to mischief. They like to pull, push, take apart, smell, taste, throw—every part of their surroundings.

There's no doubt they can try the patience of a saint, and most of us fall short of that distinction. But I'm sure that, when my friend is able to look back on it, she'll be thankful to God for all that abundant energy.

So different from the experience of another friend, whose fourth child was born with serious brain damage. At first they didn't realize the extent of his injuries, but she would say, over and over—he was such a *good* baby. Set down in one position, he would scarcely move; his head did not turn to follow his mother's face. Her anxious eyes failed to hold his attention.

There was something very wrong with that still, quiet, 'good' baby. Whereas every noisy, naughty, lively child is as natural as can be.

And is there anything more marvellous, at the end of an exhausting day, than the sight of a sleeping toddler, chubby fingers spread on pillow—limbs as relaxed as a kitten, expression as innocent as can be? There's nothing quite like the deep peace of a household when the young ones are all safe and sound—and fast asleep!

The eternal God is your dwelling place, and underneath are the everlasting arms.
Deuteronomy 33:27

We give you thanks, Lord, for all the abundance of life around us. Keep us from all fear. We rest in the security of your love.